Guitar Chord Songbook

Bluegrass

T0057753

ISBN 978-1-4584-1660-5

HAL•LEONARD®
CORPORATION

7777 W. BLUEMOUND RD. P.O. BOX 13819 MILWAUKEE, WI 53213

Visit Hal Leonard Online at
www.halleonard.com

Guitar Chord Songbook

ontents

Angel Band

Words and Music by
Ralph Stanley

Melody:

My lat - est sun __ is

(Capo 4th fret)

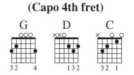

G   D   C

Intro | G | D | G | | |

Verse 1

        G   **C**   **G**
My latest sun is sinking fast,

           D **G**
My race is nearly run.

               C   **G**
My strongest trials now are past,

          D   **G**
My triumph has be - gun.

Chorus 1

D   G
Oh, come, angel band,

D   G
Come and a - round me stand.

    C   G
Oh, bear me away on your snow white wings

         D   G
To my im - mortal home.

    C   G
Oh, bear me away on your snow white wings,

         D   G
To my im - mortal home.

Verse 2

    G   C   G
Oh, bear my longing heart to Him,

        D   G
Who bled and died for me.

                  C   G
Whose blood now cleanses from all sin,

        D   G
And gives me victo - ry.

Chorus 2   *Repeat Chorus 1*

Ballad of Jed Clampett

from the Television Series
THE BEVERLY HILLBILLIES

Words and Music by
Paul Henning

Come and lis-ten to my sto-ry 'bout a

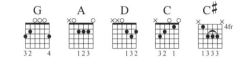

Intro | G | | | |

Verse 1
                 G   A   D
Come and listen to my story 'bout a man named Jed,

                         G
Poor mountaineer, barely kept his fam'ly fed.

                  C   C♯
Then one day he was shootin' at some food,

    D   G
And up through the ground came a bubblin' crude.

Spoken: Oil that is! Black gold, Texas tea!

GUITAR CHORD SONGBOOK

Verse 2

         G   A   D
Well, the first thing you know old Jed's a million-aire,

           G
Kin folk said, "Jed, move away from there."

             C   C♯
They said, "California's the place you oughta be."

       D   G
So they loaded up the truck and they moved to Bever - ly.

Spoken: Hills, that is! Swimmin' pools, movie stars!

Verse 3

G   A   D
Now it's time to say goodbye to Jed and all his kin.

                 G
They would like to thank you folks for kindly droppin' in.

                   C   C♯
You're all invited back next week to this locali - ty

       D   G
To have a heapin' helpin' of their hospitali - ty.

Spoken: Beverly hillbillies, that's what they call them now.

Nice folks. Y'all come back, now, y'hear?

Big Spike Hammer

Words and Music by
Bobby Osborne and Pete Goble

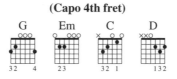

Melody:

Can't you hear the rip - ple of __

(Capo 4th fret)

G   Em   C   D

Verse 1

               G   **Em**
Can't you hear the ripple of my ___ big spike hammer?

C   **Em**
   Lord, it's bustin' my side.

              G   **Em**
I've done all I can do to keep that woman,

C   **Em**   **D**
   Still she's not satis - fied.

Chorus 1

              G
Hey, hey, Della Mae,

                     D   **G**
Why do you treat me this a way?

Hey, hey, Della Mae,

             D   **G**
I'll get even some day.

Verse 2

          G   Em
I'm the best hammer swinger in this big section gang,

C   Em
  Big Bill Johnson is my name.

            G   Em
This spike hammer that I swing for a dollar and a half a day,

  C   Em D
It's all for my Della Mae.

Chorus 2   *Repeat Chorus 1*

Verse 3

          G   Em
Well, I've been lots of places, there's not much I ain't done;

C   Em
  Still a lot of things I'd like to see.

          G   Em
Big spike hammer that I swing or the woman that I love,

    C   Em D
Yeah, one's gonna be the death of me.

Chorus 3   *Repeat Chorus 1*

Outro

Em
  Big spike hammer.

              D   G
Big spike hammer.

Blue Moon of Kentucky

Words and Music by
Bill Monroe

Melody:

Blue moon of Ken - tuck-y

(Capo 4th fret)

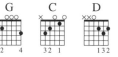

Intro

| G | | | C | | | |
| G | | D | | G | | | |

Chorus

G   C
Blue moon of Kentucky keep on shinin'.

          G   D
Shine on ____ the one that's gone and proved un - true.

          G   C
Blue moon of Kentucky keep on shinin'.

          G   D   G
Shine on ____ the one that's gone and left me blue.

Verse

G7   C   G
   It was on a moonlight night, the stars were shinin' bright,

          C   G   D
And they whispered from on high, your love has said good - bye.

          G   C
Blue moon of Kentucky keep on shinin',

          G   D   G
Shine on ____ the one that's gone and said good - bye.

How Mountain Girls Can Love

Words and Music by
Ruby Rakes

Melody:

Get down,   boys,   go back

(Capo 2nd fret)

C   G   D

32 1   32   4   1 3 2

Chorus 1

     C   G
Get down, boys, go back home,
     D   G
Back to the girl you love.
     C   G
Treat her right, never wrong,
     D   G
How mountain gals can love.

Verse 1

           G
Ridin' the night in the high, cold wind
           D   G
On the trail of the old lonesome pine.

Thinkin' of you, feelin' so blue,
           D   G
Wonderin' why I left you be - hind.

Chorus 2

Repeat Chorus 1

Verse 2

         G
Re - member the night we strolled down the lane,
     D   G
Our hearts were gay and happy then.

You whispered to me when I held you close,
     D   G
We hoped that night would never end.

Chorus 3

Repeat Chorus 1

Blue Ridge Cabin Home

Words and Music by
Louise Certain and Gladys Stacey

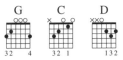

(Capo 2nd fret)

G   C   D

Verse 1

          G   **C**
There's a well beaten path on this old ____ mountain side

     D   **G**
Where I wandered when I was a lad.

                    C
There I wandered alone to the place I call home

     D   **G**
In those Blue Ridge hills far away.

Chorus 1

         G   **C**
Oh, I love those hills of old Vir - ginia,

        D   **G**
From those Blue Ridge hills I did roam.

                         C
When I die, won't you bury me in the moun - tain,

     D   **G**
Far a - way near my Blue Ridge mountain home.

GUITAR CHORD SONGBOOK

Verse 2	G C
	Now my thoughts wander back to the ram - shackle shack
	D G
	In those Blue Ridge hills far away.
	C
	My mother and dad were laid there to rest,
	D G
	They are sleeping in peace together there.

Chorus 2 *Repeat Chorus 1*

Verse 3

G   C
I re - turn to that old cabin home ___ with a sigh,

D   G
I've been longing for days gone by.

C
When I die won't you bury me on that old mountain side,

D   G
Make my resting place upon the hill so high.

Chorus 3 *Repeat Chorus 1*

BLUEGRASS

Blue Train

Words and Music by
Dave Allen

Melody:

I heard that whis - tle when I

(Capo 2nd fret)

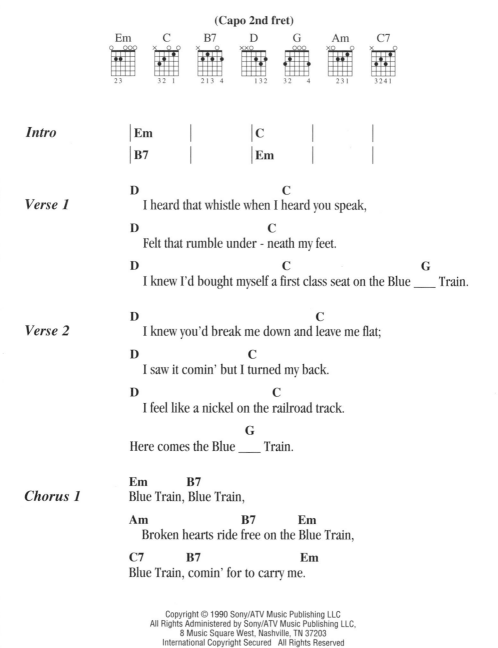

Em   C   B7   D   G   Am   C7

Intro

|Em | |C | | |
|B7 | |Em | | |

Verse 1

        D   C
I heard that whistle when I heard you speak,

        D   C
Felt that rumble under - neath my feet.

        D   C   G
I knew I'd bought myself a first class seat on the Blue ____ Train.

Verse 2

        D   C
I knew you'd break me down and leave me flat;

        D   C
I saw it comin' but I turned my back.

        D   C
I feel like a nickel on the railroad track.

                              G
Here comes the Blue ____ Train.

Chorus 1

Em   B7
Blue Train, Blue Train,

    Am   B7   Em
Broken hearts ride free on the Blue Train,

C7   B7   Em
Blue Train, comin' for to carry me.

Instrumental	‖: D			C			
(Verse)	|D			|C			
	|D			|C			
	|G			:‖			

Instrumental	|Em			|B7			
(Chorus)	|Am			|B7			
	|Em			|C7			
	|B7			|Em			

Verse 3

D   C
It's not the first time I've been down this line;

D   C
I've done some travelin' with this heart of mine.

D   C   G
Seems to be a longer ride each time on the Blue ___ Train.

Verse 4

D   C
When I get home, I'm gonna lock my heart,

D   C
Try and turn away the wounded part.

D   C
I'm gonna get myself a good head start

                      G
And out run the Blue ___ Train.

Chorus 2   *Repeat Chorus 1*

Instrumental	|Em			|B7			
	|Am			|B7			

Outro

Em   C7
Blue Train, Blue Train,

B7   Em
Comin' for to carry me ___ on the Blue Train.

Bringing Mary Home

Words and Music by Chaw Mank,
Joe Kingston and John Duffey

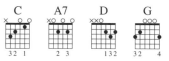

Intro | C | A7 | D | G |

Verse 1

G   D   C   G
I was driving down a lonely road on a dark and stormy night,

         D   C   D
When a little girl by the roadside showed up in my head - lights.

 G   D
I stopped and she got in back, and in a shaky tone,

     C   A7   D   G
She said, "My name is Mary, please won't you take me home."

Verse 2

       D   C   G
She must have been so frightened all a - lone there in the night.

       D
There was something strange about her,

       C   D
'Cause her face was deathly white.

   G   D
She sat so pale and quiet in the back seat all a - lone.

   C   A7   D   G
I never will for - get that night I took Mary home.

Instrumental *Repeat Intro*

Verse 3

   D   C   G
I pulled into the driveway where she told me to go.

         D   C   D
Got out to help her from the car, and opened up the door

    G   D
But I just could not believe my eyes 'cause the backseat was bare.

    G   A7   D   G
I looked all around the car, but Mary wasn't there.

Verse 4

   D   C   G
A light shone from the porch, someone opened up the door.

   D   C   D
I asked about the little girl that I was looking for.

     G   D
Then the lady gently smiled, and brushed a tear a - way.

    C   A7   D   G
She said, "It sure was nice of you to go out of your way."

Verse 5

   D   C   G
Thirteen years ago today, in a wreck just down the road,

        D   C   D
Our darling Mary lost her life, and we miss her so.

    G   D
Oh, thank you for your trouble and the kindness you have shown.

      C   A7   D   G
You're the thirteenth one who's been here bringing Mary home.

Outro |C |A7 |D |G | ‖

Cash on the Barrelhead

Words and Music by
Charles Louvin and Ira Louvin

Got in ___ a lit - tle trou - ble ___

(Capo 3rd fret)

A   D   G

Intro |A | |D | |

Verse 1
                  D
Got in a little trouble at the county seat.

                                    A   **D**
Lord, they put me in the jailhouse for loafing on the street.

When the judge heard the verdict, I was a guilty man.

                              A   **D**
He said, "Forty-five dollars or thirty day in the can."

Chorus 1
              G   **D**
That'll be cash on the barrelhead, son.

                    A   **D**
You can take your choice, you're twenty - one.

              G   **D**
No money down, no credit plan.

              A   **D**
No time to chase you, 'cause I'm a busy man.

Verse 2

                D
Found a telephone number on a laundry slip.

                A   D
I had a good-hearted jailer with a six-gun hip.

He let me call long distance; she said, "Number, please."

                A   D
No sooner had I told her, she shouted out at me.

Chorus 2

        G   D
That'll be cash on the barrelhead, son.

        A   D
Not part, not half, but the entire sum.

        G   D
No money down, no credit plan,

        A   D
'Cause the little bird tells me that you're a trav'lin' man.

Verse 3

                D
Thirty day in the jailhouse four days on the road.

                A   D
I was feelin' mighty hungry, my feet a heavy load.

I saw a Greyhound a comin', stuck up my thumb.

                A   D
Just as I was being seated, the driver caught my arm.

Chorus 3

        G   D
That'll be cash on the barrelhead, son.

        A   D
This old grey dog gets paid to run.

        G   D
When the engine starts and the wheels won't roll,

        A   D
Give me cash on the barrelhead, I'll take you down the road.

Dark Hollow

Words and Music by
Bill Browning

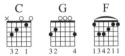

Verse 1

        C **G**   **C**
I'd rather be in some dark hollow

                F **C**
Where the sun don't ever shine,

                      F
Than to be in some big city

        C   **G**   **C**
In a small room with you on my mind.

Chorus 1

       C   **G**   **C**
So blow your whistle freight train,

                F   **C**
Carry me farther on down the track.

                F
I'm going away, I'm leaving today.

       C   **G**   **C**
I'm going but I ain't coming back.

Verse 2

                    C   G   C
          I'd rather be in some dark hollow

                        F   C
          Where the sun don't ever shine,

                              F
          Than to be at home alone knowing that you're gone,

                    C   G   C
          It would cause me to lose my mind.

Chorus 2   *Repeat Chorus 1*

                    C   F
Outro   I'm going away, I'm leaving today,

                    C   G   C
          I'm going but I ain't coming back.

Doin' My Time

Words and Music by
Jimmie Skinner

On this old __ rock pile, _____

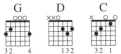

Intro

N.C.	G				
	D	G			
				D	
G					

Verse 1

G
On this old rock pile, with a ball and chain,

                                D   G
They call me by a number, not a name, ___ Lord, Lord.

Chorus 1

                 C   G
Gotta do my time, gotta do my time,

                 D   G
With an aching heart and a worried mind.

Instrumental 1 |G | | |
                      | | |D |
                      |G | | |

Verse 2

G
   When that old judge looked down and smiled,

                                        D   G
   He said, "I'll put you on that good road for a while,"___ Lord, Lord.

Chorus 2   *Repeat Chorus 1*

Instrumental 2   *Repeat Instrumental 1*

Verse 3

G
   You can hear my hammer, you can hear my song.

                                  D   G
   I'm gonna swing it like John Henry all day long, ___ Lord, Lord.

Chorus 3   *Repeat Chorus 1*

Instrumental 3   *Repeat Instrumental 1*

Verse 4

G
   It won't be long, just a few more days.

                           D   G
   I'll settle down and quit my rowdy ways, ___ Lord, Lord.

Chorus 4

G   C   G
With that gal of mine, ___ with that gal of mine.
                        D   G
She'll be waiting for me when I've done my time.

Dooley

Words by Mitchell F. Jayne
Music by Rodney Dillard

(Capo 4th fret)

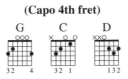

Verse 1

G   C   G   D
Dooley was a good old man; he lived below the mill.

G   C   G D G
Dooley had two daughters and a forty gallon still.

                  C   G   D
One gal watched the boiler, the other watched the spout,

     G   C   G D   G
And mama caught the bottles when old Dooley fetched them out.

Chorus 1

G
Dooley, slippin' up the holler,

C
Dooley, tryin' to make a dollar.

G
   Dooley, give me a swaller

     D   G
And I'll pay you back some day.

GUITAR CHORD SONGBOOK

Verse 2

```
     G        C        G             D
The revenuers came for him, slippin' through the woods,
     G           C          G    D    G
But Dooley kept be - hind them all and never lost his goods.
               C        G          D
Dooley was a trader when into town he'd come.
     G        C         G    D       G
Sugar by the bushel and mo - lasses by the drum.
```

Chorus 2   *Repeat Chorus 1*

Verse 3

```
     G        C        G          D
I remember very well the day old Dooley died.
     G              C          G      D      G
The women folk looked sorry and the men stood 'round and cried.
               C        G            D
Now Dooley's on the mountain; he lies there all a - lone.
     G        C         G    D    G
They put a jug be - side him and a barrel for his stone.
```

Chorus 3

```
     G
Dooley, slippin' up the holler,
     C
Dooley, tryin' to make a dollar.
     G
  Dooley, give me a swaller
          D              G
And I'll pay you back some day.
          D              G
And I'll pay you back some day.
```

Outro | G | C | D | G   ‖

Down the Road

By Lester Flatt and
Earl Scruggs

Now   down   the   road _   just   a   mile

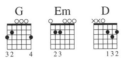

Verse 1

G		Em

Now down the road just a mile or two

G   **D**   **G**
Lives a little girl named Pearly Blue.

                                    Em
About so high and her hair was brown,

G   **D**   **G**
The prettiest thing boys, in this town.

Verse 2

G   **Em**
Now any time you want to know

G   **D**   **G**
Where I'm going down the road

                            Em
Get my girl on the line

G   **D**   **G**
You'll find me there most any old time.

Verse 3	G Em Now every day and Sunday too

      G   D   G
I go to see my Pearly Blue.

                            Em
Before you hear that rooster crow

      G   D   G
You'll see me headed down the road.

Verse 4

    G   Em
Now old man Flatt he owned the farm

G   D   G
From the hog lot to the barn.

                  Em
From the barn to the rail

    G   D   G
He made his living by carrying the mail.

Verse 5

    G   Em
Now every time I get the blues

    G   D   G
I walk the soles right off my shoes.

                    Em
I don't know why I love her so,

    G   D   G
That gal of mine lives down the road.

Verse 6   *Repeat Verse 1*

Foggy Mountain Top

Words and Music by A.P. Carter,
Maybelle Carter and Sara Carter

Melody:

If I was on some _

(Capo 2nd fret)

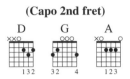

D G A

Chorus 1	**D** **G** **D** If I was on some foggy mountain top,

Chorus 1

               D   **G**   **D**
If I was on some foggy mountain top,

                        A
I'd sail away to the west.

               D   **G**   **D**
I'd sail all around this whole wide world

                    A   **D**
To the girl I love the best.

Verse 1

               D   **G** **D**
Now, if I had listened to what mama said,

                        A
I would not be here to - day

         D   **G**   **D**
A lyin' around this old jail - house

                   A   **D**
A weeping my sweet life a - way.

Chorus 2	*Repeat Chorus 1*

Verse 2
```
            D                 G     D
When - ever you see that girl of mine,

                         A
There's something you can tell her;

            D                G      D
That she need not to fool her time a - way

              A     D
Just to court some other feller.
```

Verse 3
```
            D                     G            D
She caused me to weep and she caused me to mourn;

                         A
She caused me to leave my home.

            D                   G      D
To them lonesome pines and them good old times

              A        D
I'm on my way back home.
```

Chorus 3	*Repeat Chorus 1*

Verse 4
```
            D       G     D
When - ever you go a courtin', boys,

                    A
Let me tell you how to do;

            D         G      D
Pull off that longtail rousta - bout;

            A    D
Put on your navy blue.
```

Chorus 4	*Repeat Chorus 1*

Footprints in the Snow

Words and Music by
Rupert Jones

Some folks like the sum-mer-time ___

(Capo 2nd fret)

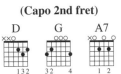

D   G   A7

Verse 1

D   G
Some folks like the summertime when they can walk a - bout,

A7   D
Strolling through the meadow green is pleasant there's no doubt.

                                       G
But give me the wintertime when the snow is on the ground,

      A7   D
For I found her when the snow was on the ground.

Chorus 1

      D   A7
I traced her little footprints in the snow,

                       D
I found her little footprints in the snow, Lord.

              G
Bless that happy day that Nellie lost her way,

    A7   D
For I found her when the snow was on the ground.

	D **G**
Verse 2	I dropped in to see her, there was a big round moon,

        A7   **D**

Her mother said she just stepped out but'd be returning soon.

                                                     G

I found her little footprints, and I traced them through the snow,

        A7   **D**

And I found her when the snow was on the ground.

Chorus 2	*Repeat Chorus 1*

	D **G**
Verse 3	Now she's up in heaven, she's with an angel band,

        A7   **D**

I know I'm going to meet her in that promised land.

                                                     G

But ev'rytime the snow falls, it brings back memories,

        A7   **D**

For I found her when the snow was on the ground.

Chorus 3	*Repeat Chorus 1*

Fox on the Run

Words and Music by
Tony Hazzard

Melody:

She walks through the corn lead-ing

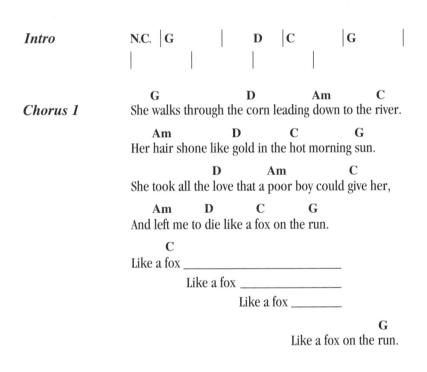

(Capo 4th fret)

G   D   C   Am   A7

Intro

N.C. | G | D | C | G |
| | | |

Chorus 1

     G   **D**   **Am**   **C**
She walks through the corn leading down to the river.

    Am   **D**   **C**   **G**
Her hair shone like gold in the hot morning sun.

              D   **Am**   **C**
She took all the love that a poor boy could give her,

  Am   **D**   **C**   **G**
And left me to die like a fox on the run.

     C
Like a fox _____

        Like a fox _____

           Like a fox _____

                  G
Like a fox on the run.

	G D G
Verse 1	Now, ev'rybody knows the reason for the fall

                              C   G   A7   D

When woman tempted man down in paradise's hall.

                              C   G   D   G

This woman tempted me, and took me for a ride.

                              C   G   D   G

Now like a lonely fox, I need a place to hide.

Chorus 2	*Repeat Chorus 1*

	G D G
Verse 2	We'll pour a glass of wine to fortify our souls.

                              C   G   A7   D

We'll talk about the world and friends we used to know.

                            C   G   D   G

I see a string of girls who'll put me on the floor,

                              C   G   D   G

The game is nearly over and the hounds are at my door.

Chorus 3	*Repeat Chorus 1*

Freeborn Man

Words and Music by
Keith Allison and Mark Lindsay

Melody:

I was born in the south - land _____

(Capo 2nd fret)

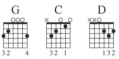

G C D

Verse 1

        G
I was born in the southland

Twenty some odd years ago.

I ran away for the first time

When I was four years old.

Chorus 1

               C   G
I'm a freeborn man; my home is on my back.

      D   G
I know every inch of highway, and every foot of back road

Every mile of railroad track.

Verse 2

        G
I got a gal in Cincinnati,

Got a woman in San Anton'.

I always loved the girl next door,

But any place is home.

Chorus 2   *Repeat Chorus 1*

Instrumental 1

‖: G | | | :‖
C			G
	D		
	G		

Verse 3

G
I got me a worn-out guitar

I carry in an old tote sack.

I hocked it about two hundred times,

But I always get it back.

Chorus 3   *Repeat Chorus 1*

Instrumental 2   *Repeat Instrumental 1*

Verse 4

G
You may not like my appearance,

And may not like my song.

You may not like the way I talk,

But you'll like the way I'm gone.

Chorus 4   *Repeat Chorus 1*

Ginseng Sullivan

Words and Music by
Norman Blake

Melody:

A - bout three miles _ from the   Bat - elle _

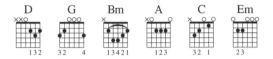

D   G   Bm   A   C   Em

Verse 1

        D
A - bout three miles from the Batelle yards

            G
From the reverse curve on down,

       D
Not far south of the town depot,

G   **Bm**
Sullivan's shack was found

A   **D**
Back on higher ground.

Verse 2

    D
You could see him ev'ry day

         G
Walking down the line,

               D
With his old brown sack across ___ his back

    G   **Bm**
And his long hair down be - hind,

A   **D**
Speaking his worried mind.

Chorus 1

       D   **G**
It's a long way to the Delta from the North Georgia hills,

                  D   **G**
And a tote sack full of gin - seng won't pay no traveling bills.

        C   **D**   **Em**   **A**
And I'm ___ too old to ride the rails or thumb the road alone.

      D   **G**   **D**
Well, I guess I'll never make ___ it back to home;

           G   **A**   **D**
My muddy water Mississippi Delta home.

Verse 3

         D
Well, the winters here, they get too cold;

         G
The damp, it makes me ill.

              D
You can't dig no roots in the mountainside

      G   **Bm**
Where the ground froze hard and still.

      A   **D**
You gotta stay at the foot of the hill.

Verse 4

  D
But next summer if things turn right,

             G
The companies will pay high.

             D
I'll make enough money to pay my bills

  G   **Bm**
And bid these mountains good - bye.

 A   **D**
Then he said with a sigh…

Chorus 2   *Repeat Chorus 1*

Green Light on the Southern

Words and Music by
Norman Blake

Melody:

Stand - ing   on   the   side ___   track

(Capo 2nd fret)

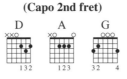

Verse 1

    D   A   D
Standing on the side track at the south end of town

                                 A
On a dry, hot, dusty August day, the steam pipe blowin' down.

    D   A   D
The fireman with his long oil can a oiling the old valve gears,

                           A   D
Waiting for the fast mail train the semaphore to clear.

Verse 2

    D   A   D
The engineer in the old high cab, his gold watch in his hand,

                       A
Looking at the water glass and lettin' down the sand.

D   A   D
Rolling out on the old main line, takin' up the slack;

                       A   D
Gone today but, so they say, to - morrow he'll be back.

	D A G D
Chorus 1	Oh, if I could re turn

        G   D   A
To those boyhood days of mine

        D
And that green light on the Southern,

          A D
Southern Rail - road line.

Verse 3

    D   A   D
Creepin' down the rusty rails on the weed-grown branch line;

                      A
Section houses gray and white by the yard limit sign.

      D   A   D
The hoggers call the old highball, no more time to wait.

                      A   D
Rolling down to Birmingham with a ten car local freight.

Verse 4

    D   A   D
The whistles scream with a hiss of steam, the headlight gleams clear;

                      A
The drivers roll on the green and go getting mighty near.

    D   A   D
Handing up the orders to the engine crew on time;

                      A   D
It's the Alabama Great Southern AG - S Railroad line.

Chorus 2   *Repeat Chorus 1*

Head Over Heels in Love with You
(I'm Head Over Heels in Love)

Words and Music by
Lester Flatt

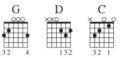

Verse 1

       G
I think I'll go across the ocean if I don't change my notion,

         D   **G**
I've just got to forget ____ you if I can.

Chorus 1

     C
Oh, I'm feel - in' so blue,

 G
I don't know what to do,

       D   **G**
For I'm head over heels in love with you.

Instrumental 1   *Repeat Verse 1 & Chorus 1*

Verse 2

     G
Ev'ry day is sad an' lonely for I'm thinkin' of you only,

        D   **G**
Oh, I just can't sleep ____ when I lay down.

Chorus 2   *Repeat Chorus 1*

Instrumental 2   *Repeat Verse 1 & Chorus 1*

	G
Verse 3	Oh, the nights are long and dreary, all I do is sit and worry,

D   **G**

I just can't bear the thought ___ of losing you.

Chorus 3   *Repeat Chorus 1*

Instrumental 3   *Repeat Verse 1 & Chorus 1*

                              G

Verse 4   Oh, I like to be forgivin' but this life ain't worth livin'

                         D   **G**

If I have to sit and wor - ry over you.

Chorus 4   *Repeat Chorus 1*

Instrumental 4

G				
	D	G		
C		G		

       G   **D**   **G**

Outro   For I'm head over heels in love with you.

High on a Mountain Top

Words and Music by
Ola Belle Reed

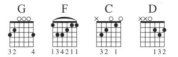

Chorus 1

    G   F   G   C
High on a mountain top,   standing all alone,

G   D   G
Wond'ring where all the years ___ of my life have flown.

          F   G   C
High on a mountain top,   wind blowing free,

G   D   G
Thinking about the days ___ that used to be.

Verse 1

    G   F   G
   As I looked in that valley down below,

              F   G
It was green just as far as I could see.

                      F   G   C
As my memory returned, ___ oh, how my heart did yearn

G   D   G
For you and the days that used to be.

GUITAR CHORD SONGBOOK

Chorus 2   *Repeat Chorus 1*

                    G   F   G

Verse 2   Well, I wonder if you ever think of me,

                                 F   G

           Or has time blotted out your memo - ry?

                                  F   G   C

           As I listen to the breeze whisper gently to the trees,

                    G   D   G

           I'll always cherish what you meant to me.

Chorus 3   *Repeat Chorus 1*

                    G   D   G

Outro   I wonder if you ever think of me.

I Ain't Goin' to Work Tomorrow

Words and Music by A.P. Carter,
Lester Flatt and Earl Scruggs

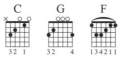

Verse 1

        C
Oh, I'm gonna leave this country, Lord,

      G   **C**
I'm gonna leave this world.

      F   **C**
Oh, I'm gonna leave this country

         G   **C**
For the sake of one little girl.

Chorus 1

        C
Oh, I ain't gonna work tomorrow,

      G   **C**
I ain't gonna work next day.

      F   **C**
Lord, I ain't gonna work to - morrow,

        G   **C**
For it may be a rainy day.

Verse 2

                C
Can't you hear that banjo ringing,

                     G   C
Can't you hear that mournful sound.

                F   C
Can't you hear those pretty girls laughin',

                  G   C
Over on the cold, cold ground.

Chorus 2   *Repeat Chorus 1*

Verse 3

              C
Oh, I'll hang my head in sorrow,

                  G   C
Lord, I'll hang my head and cry.

              F   C
Oh, I'll hang my head in sorrow,

                  G   C
As my darlin' passes by.

Chorus 3   *Repeat Chorus 1*

I Am a Man of Constant Sorrow

Words and Music by
Carter Stanley

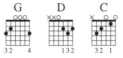

Intro

       G   D   G
In constant sorrow all my days.

Verse 1

      G   C
I am a man of constant sorrow,

            D   G
I've seen trouble all my days.

                    C
I bid farewell to old Ken - tucky,

               D   G
The state where I was borned and raised.

               D   G
(The state where he was borned and raised.)

Verse 2

      G   C
For six long years I've been in trouble,

           D   G
No pleasure here on earth I find.

                      C
For in this world I'm bound to ramble,

           D   G
I have no friends to help me now.

           D   G
(He has no friends to help him now.)

Verse 3

```
G                              C
You can bury me in some deep valley,
        D                  G
For many years where I may lay.
                           C
Then you may learn to love an - other
        D             G
While I am sleeping in my grave.
        D             G
(While he is sleeping in his grave.)
```

Verse 4

```
G                              C
Maybe your friends think I'm just a stranger,
        D             G
My face you never will see no more.
                           C
But there is one promise that is given;
        D             G
I'll meet you on God's golden shore.
        D             G
(He'll meet you on God's golden shore.)
```

I'll Fly Away

Words and Music by
Albert E. Brumley

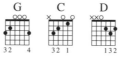

G   C   D

Verse 1

G
Some bright morning when this life is o'er,

C   G
I'll fly a - way,

To that home on God's celestial shore,

   D   G
I'll ____ fly a - way.

Chorus 1

G
I'll fly away, oh glory,

C   G
I'll fly a - way (in the morning).

When I die hallelujah by and by,

   D   G
I'll ____ fly a - way.

Verse 2

G
When the shadows of this life have gone,

C   G
I'll fly a - way,

Like a bird from these prison walls I'll fly,

     D   G
I'll ___ fly a - way.

Chorus 2   *Repeat Chorus 1*

Verse 3

G
Oh, how glad and happy when we meet,

C   G
I'll fly a - way,

No more cold darn shackles on my feet,

     D   G
I'll ___ fly a - way.

Chorus 3   *Repeat Chorus 1*

Verse 4

G
Just a few more weary days and then,

C   G
I'll fly a - way,

To a land where joys will never end,

     D   G
I'll ___ fly a - way.

Chorus 4   *Repeat Chorus 1*

I'm Blue, I'm Lonesome

Melody:

Words and Music by
Bill Monroe and Hank Williams

The lone - some sigh __

(Capo 4th fret)

G   C   D   A

Verse 1

           G   C   G
The lone - some sigh of a train going by

                  D   G
Makes me want to stop and cry.

               C   G
I recall the day it took you a - way.

           D   G
I'm blue, I'm lonesome too.

Chorus 1

D   G
When I hear the whistle blow,

A   D
I want to pack my clothes and go.

       G   D   G
The lone - some sigh of a train going by

           D   G
Makes me want to stop and cry.

Verse 2

       G   C   G
In the still of the night, in the pale moon - light,

          D   G
The winds, they moan and cry.

             C   G
These lonesome blues I just can't lose.

          D   G
I'm blue, I'm lonesome too.

Chorus 2   *Repeat Chorus 1*

Kentucky Waltz

Words and Music by
Bill Monroe

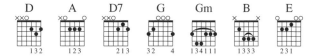

Verse

        D
We were waltzing that night in Kentucky,

           A
Beneath the beautiful harvest moon.

And I was the boy that was lucky,

        D
But it all ended too soon.

As I sit here alone in the moonlight,

  D7   **G**
I see your smiling face,

        Gm   **D**   **B**
And I long once more for your em - brace

     E   **A**   **D**
And that beautiful Ken - tucky Waltz.

If I Lose

Words and Music by
Ralph Stanley

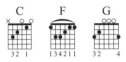

```
  C        F        G
x       o  o               o o o
• • •    • • • •      • • •
 • •      •
32  1    1 3 4 2 1 1  32      4
```

Intro
| C | | | F | | |
| G | | | C | | |

Verse 1

C   F
I never thought I'd need you, but now I find I'm wrong.

G   C
Come on back, sweet mama, back where you be - long.

                         F
I've gambled over town, find that I can't win.

G   C
Come on back and pick me up again.

Chorus 1

            G   C
Now if I lose, (If I lose) let me lose. ___ (let me lose.)

            G   C
I don't care (I don't care…) how much I lose.

                              F
If I lose a hundred dollars while I'm tryin' to win a dime,

          G   C
My baby, she's got money all the time.

Instrumental	|G		|C		|
	|G		|C		|
	|		|F		|
	|G		|C		|

Verse 2

        C   F
Of all the other gals I know, none can take your place,

            G   C
'Cause when I get into a jam, they just ain't in the race.

                                       F
So now that you're back, dear, let's make another round.

            G   C
With you here by my side, babe, my deal just can't go down.

Chorus 2   *Repeat Chorus 1*

In the Pines

Words and Music by Thomas Bryant,
Jimmie Davis and Clayton McMichen

(Capo 2nd fret)

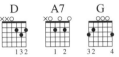

Intro |D |A7 |D | |

Verse 1
```
          D          G  D
The longest train I ever saw

               A7       D
When down that Georgia line.

               G       D
The engine passed at six o' - clock,

               A7   D
And the cab passed by at nine.
```

Chorus 1
```
          D
In the pines, in the pines,

          G         D
Where the sun never shines,

               A7         D
And we shiver when the cold winds blow.
```

Verse 2

        D   **G**   **D**
I asked my captain, for the time of day,

                    A7   **D**
He said he throwed his watch a - way.

                  G   **D**
A long steel rail and a short cross tie,

          A7   **D**
I'm on my way back home.

Chorus 2   *Repeat Chorus 1*

Verse 3

        D   **G**   **D**
Little girl, little girl, what have I done

                A7   **D**
That makes you treat me so?

                      G   **D**
You caused me to weep, you caused me to moan,

                A7   **D**
You caused me to leave my home.

Chorus 3   *Repeat Chorus 1*

Keep on the Sunny Side

Words and Music by
A.P. Carter

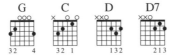

Verse 1

        G   **C**   **G**
There's a dark and a troubled side of life.

                             D
There's a bright and a sunny side too.

        D7   **G**
Though you meet with the darkness and strife,

      D   **G**
The sunny side may also find you.

Chorus 1

G   **C**   **G**
Keep on the sunny side, always on the sunny side,

                D
Keep on the sunny side of life.

      G   **C**   **G**
It will help us ev'ry day, it will brighten all the way

        C   **G**   **D**   **G**
If we keep on the sunny side of life.

Verse 2	G C G Oh, the storm and its fury broke to - day,

                                     D
Crushing hopes that we cherish so dear.

          D7   G
Clouds and storms will in time pass a - way;

         D   G
The sun again will shine bright and clear.

Chorus 2   *Repeat Chorus 1*

Verse 3
         G   C   G
Let us greet with a song of hope each day,

                                 D
Though the moment be cloudy or fair.

         D7   G
Let us trust in our Savior a - way,

         D   G
Who keepeth ev'ryone in His care.

Chorus 3   *Repeat Chorus 1*

The Long Black Veil

Words and Music by
Marijohn Wilkin and Danny Dill

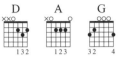

Verse 1

D
Ten years ago on a cold, dark night,

                      A   G   D
There was some - one killed 'neath the town ___ hall light.

The people that saw, they all agreed

                      A   G   D
That the slayer who ran looked a lot ___ like me.

Verse 2

D
The judge said, "Son, what is your alibi?

                     A   G   D
If you were some - where else, then you won't have to die."

I spoke not a word, though it meant my life,

                   A   G   D
For I had been in the arms of my best friend's wife.

Chorus 1

G	D	G	D

She walks these hills in a long black veil.

G	D	G	D

She visits my grave when the night winds wail.

           G   A   D

Nobody knows, nobody sees, nobody knows ___ but me.

Verse 3

D

The scaffold was high, and eternity near.

A   G   D

She stood in the crowd, and shed not a tear.

And sometimes at night when the cold winds moan,

A   G   D

In a long black veil she cries o'er my bones.

Chorus 2   *Repeat Chorus 1*

Midnight Moonlight

Words and Music by
Peter Rowan

(Capo 2nd fret)

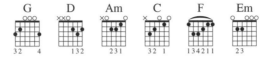

Verse 1

    G
If you ever feel lonesome

D
And you're down in San Anton',

Am   **D**   **C**
Beg, steal or borrow two nickels or a dime

                F
And call me on the phone.

    G
I'll meet you at Alamo Mission,

D
Where we can say our prayers.

Am   **D**
The Holy Ghost and the Virgin Mother

         Em   **D**   **C**
Will heal us ____ as we kneel ____ there.

Chorus 1

        F   C   F
In the moonlight,   in the midnight,

C   F   C   G
In the moonlight, midnight moon - light.

        F   C   F
In the moonlight,   in the midnight,

C   F   C   G
In the moonlight, midnight moon - light.

Verse 2

G
If you ever feel sorrow

D
For the deeds you have done,

Am   D
With no hope for to - morrow,

C   F
In the setting of the sun.

G
And the ocean is howling

D
For things that might have been

Am   D
That lost good morning sunrise

          Em   D   C
Will be the brightest you've ever seen.

Chorus 2   *Repeat Chorus 1*

Molly and Ten Brooks

Words and Music by
Bill Monroe

Melody:

Run old   Mol - ly   run, ___

(Capo 4th fret)

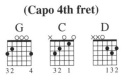

Verse 1

    G   C
Run old Molly run, run old Molly run,

            G   D   G
Ten brooks gonna beat you to the bright shinin' sun.

                                  D   G
To the bright shining sun, oh Lord, to the bright shining sun.

Verse 2

    G   C
Tenbrooks was a Big Bay horse, he wore a shaggy mane.

            G   D   G
He run all around Memphis, he beat the Memphis train.

                              D   G
Beat the Memphis train, oh Lord, beat the Memphis train.

Verse 3

```
G                                              C
Tenbrooks said to Molly, what makes your head so red?

        G              D         G
Running in the hot sun with a fever in my head.

                      D         G
Fever in my head, oh Lord, fever in my head.
```

Verse 4

```
G                                              C
Molly said to Tenbrooks, you're looking mighty squirrel.

            G         D         G
Tenbrooks said to Molly, I'm leaving this old world.

D         G
Leaving this old world.
```

Verse 5

```
G                                          C
Out in California where Molly done as she pleased,

                  G              D         G
She came back to old Kentucky got beat with all ease.

D         G
Beat with all ease.
```

Verse 6

```
G                                          C
Women's all a laughin', children's all a cryin',

            G         D         G
Men's all a hollerin', old Tenbrooks is flyin',

        D         G
Old Tenbrooks is flyin'.
```

Verse 7

```
G                                    C
Kaiper, Kaiper you're not ridin' right.

                    G
Molly's a beatin' old Tenbrooks.

D        G   D        G
Clear out of sight, clear out of sight.
```

Verse 8

```
G                          C
Kaiper, Kaiper, Kaiper my son

                      G
Give old Tenbrooks the bridle

      D            G   D            G
And let old Tenbrooks run. Let old Tenbrooks run.
```

Verse 9

```
G                                                   C
Go and fetch old Tenbrooks and hitch him in the shade.

                        G        D        G
We're gonna bury old Molly in a coffin ready-made.

      D        G
In a coffin ready-made.
```

Outro

```
|G        |         |        |C        |
|         |G        |D       |G        |
```

```
G
Let old Tenbrooks run, oh Lord,

D            G        D  G
Let old Tenbrooks run.
```

More Pretty Girls Than One

American Folk Song

Melody:

There's more pret-ty girls

C   G   F

32 1   32   4   1 3 4 2 1 1

Chorus 1

      C   G   C
There's more pretty girls than one,
F   C
More pretty girls than one.
F   C
Any old town that I ramble around in
       G   C
There's more pretty girls than one.

Verse 1

C   G C
Mama talked to me ___ last night;
   F   C
She gave to me some good ad - vice.
     F   C
She said, "Son you ought to quit this old rambling all around
         G   C
And marry you a sweet ___ loving wife."

Chorus 2

Repeat Chorus 1

Verse 2

C   G   C
 Honey, look down that old lonesome road;
   F   C
Hang down your pretty head and cry.
     F   C
'Cause I'm thinking all about them pretty little girls,
      G C
And hoping that I'll never die.

Chorus 3

Repeat Chorus 1

Nellie Kane

Words and Music by
Tim O'Brien

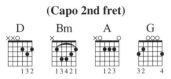

Melody:

As a young _ man

(Capo 2nd fret)

D   Bm   A   G

Verse 1

                  D
As a young ____ man I went ridin' out on the Western plain.

                                      Bm
In the state of North Dakota I met my Nellie Kane,

A   **D**
I met my Nellie Kane.

Verse 2

          D
She was livin' in a lonely cabin with a son by another man.

                                        Bm
Five years she had waited for him, as long as a woman can,

A   **D**
Long as a woman can.

Chorus 1

          G   **D**
I don't know what changed my mind;

              A   **D**
'Till then I was the ramblin' kind.

          G   **D**
A kind of love I can't ex - plain

          A   **D**
That I have for Nellie Kane.

Verse 3
D
She took me on to work that day to help her till the land.

                                                      Bm
In the afternoon we planted seeds, in the evening we held hands,

A   **D**
In the evening we held hands.

Verse 4
D
Her blue eyes told me everything a man could want to know,

                             Bm
And it was then I realized I would never go,

A   **D**
I would never go.

Chorus 2   *Repeat Chorus 1*

Verse 5
D
Now many years have gone by and the son has grown up tall.

                                    Bm
I became a father to him and she became my all,

A   **D**
She became my all.

Chorus 3
           G   **D**
I don't know what changed my mind;

                  A   **D**
'Till then I was the ramblin' kind.

           G   **D**
A kind of love I can't ex - plain

                  A   **D**
That I have for Nellie Kane,

                  A   **D**
That I have for Nellie Kane.

Old Home Place

Words by Mitchell F. Jayne
Music by Rodney Dillard

Melody:

It's been   ten   long years

(Capo 2nd fret)

G   B7   C   D   A7

Verse 1

       G   B7   C   G
It's been ten long years since I left my home

                    D
In the hollow where I was born.

       G   B7   C   G
Where the cool fall nights made the wood smoke rise,

           D   G
And the fox hunter blew his horn.

Verse 2

       G B7   C   G
I fell in love with a girl in the town.

                   D
I thought that she would be true.

       G   B7 C   G
I went a - way to Charlottes - ville,

           D   G
And worked in a sawmill crew.

Chorus 1

D   G
What have they done with the old home place?

A7   D
Why did they tear it down?

  G   B7 C   G
And why did I leave the plow in the fields

        D   G
And look for a job ___ in the town?

Verse 3

  G   B7 C   G
The girl ran off with somebody else.

          D
The tariffs took all my pay.

  G B7   C   G
And here I stand where the old home stood,

      D   G
Before they took it a - way.

Verse 4

     G   B7   C   G
Now the geese fly south and the wind grows cold

           D
As I stand here and hang my head.

  G   B7   C G
I've lost my love, I've lost my home,

      D   G
And now I wish that I was dead.

Chorus 2   *Repeat Chorus 1*

Panama Red

Words and Music by
Peter Rowan

Pan-a-ma Red,   Pan-a-ma

F#7 G A D Bm E7

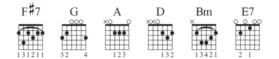

Intro | F#7 | | G | | |
          | A | | | D | |

Chorus 1
      Bm   **A**
Panama Red, Panama Red,

    G   **E7**   **A**
He'll steal your woman, then he'll rob your head.

      Bm   **A**
Panama Red, Panama Red,

    F#7   **G**
On his white horse, Mescalito, he comes ___ breezin' through town.

      A   **D**
I bet your woman's up in bed with old Panama Red.

Verse 1

        D
        The judge don't know when Red's in town;

          G
He keeps well hidden underground.

       A   **D**
Ev'ry - body's actin' lazy, fallin' out and hangin' around.

               G
My woman says, "Hey, Pedro, you're actin' crazy like a clown."

     A   **D**
No - body feels like workin'; Panama Red is back in town.

Chorus 2   *Repeat Chorus 1*

Verse 2

D   **G**
  Well, ev'rybody's lookin' out for him, 'cause they know Red satisfies;

A   **D**
  Little girls love to listen to him sing and tell sweet lies.

                 G
But when things get too confusing, honey, we're better off in bed.

     A   **D**
I'll be searchin' all the joints in town for Panama Red.

Chorus 3   *Repeat Chorus 1*

Rocky Top

Words and Music by
Boudleaux Bryant and Felice Bryant

Melody:

Wish that I was on ol' Rock-y Top,

G   C   Em   D   F

Verse 1

G   C   G
Wish that I was on ol' Rocky Top,

Em   D   G
Down in the Tennessee hills.

            C   G
Ain't no smoggy smoke on Rocky Top,

Em   D   G
Ain't no telephone bills.

Verse 2

G   C   G
Once I had a girl on Rocky Top,

Em   D   G
Half bear, the other half cat.

             C   G
Wild as a mink, but sweet as soda pop;

Em D   G
I still dream about that.

Chorus 1

Em   D
Rocky Top, you'll always be

F   C
Home sweet home to me.

         G
Good ol' Rocky Top,

        F   G
Rocky Top, Tennes-see.

        D   G
Rocky Top, Tennes-see.

Verse 3

G   C   G
Once two strangers climbed ol' Rocky Top,

Em   D   G
Lookin' for a moonshine still.

                   C   G
Strangers ain't come down from Rocky Top;

Em   D   G
Reckon they never will.

Verse 4

G   C   G
Corn won't grow at all on Rocky Top,

Em   D   G
Dirt's too rocky by far.

                  C   G
That's why all the folks on Rocky Top

Em   D   G
Get their corn from a jar.

Chorus 2   **Repeat Chorus 1**

Verse 5

G   C   G
I've had years of cramped-up city life,

Em   D   G
Trapped like a duck in a pen.

            C   G
All I know is it's a pity life

Em   D   G
Can't be simple a-gain.

Chorus 3

Em   D
Rocky Top, you'll always be

F   C
Home sweet home to me.

        G
Good ol' Rocky Top,

         F   G
Rocky Top, Tennes-see.

         D   G
Rocky Top, Tennes-see,

               F C G
Rock Top, Tennessee.

Roll in My Sweet Baby's Arms

Traditional

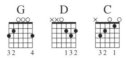

Chorus 1

G
Roll in my sweet baby's arms,

                      D
Roll in my sweet baby's arms.

G   C
Lay 'round the shack 'till the mail train comes back,

        D   G
And roll in my sweet baby's arms.

Verse 1

     G
I ain't gonna work on no railroad,

                   D
Ain't gonna work on no farm.

G   C
Lay 'round the shack 'till the mail train comes back

        D   G
And roll in my sweet baby's arms.

Chorus 2   *Repeat Chorus 1*

Verse 2

    G
Now where were you last Saturday night,

            D
While I was lying in jail?

G   **C**
Walking the streets with an - other man,

D   **G**
Wouldn't even go my bail.

Chorus 3   *Repeat Chorus 1*

Verse 3

    G
I know your parents don't like me.

               D
They throw me away from your door.

  G   **C**
If I had my life to live over,

  D   **G**
I wouldn't go there any - more.

Chorus 4   *Repeat Chorus 1*

Salty Dog Blues

Words and Music by
Wiley A. Morris and Zeke Morris

I was stand-in' on the cor-ner with the

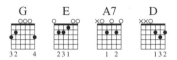

Verse 1

       G   **E**
I was standin' on the corner with the low down blues,

    A7
A great big hole in the bottom of my shoes.

D   **G**
Honey, let me be your salty dog.

Chorus 1

       G   **E**
Well, let me be your salty dog,

    A7
Or I won't be your man at all,

D   **G**
Honey, let me be your salty dog.

	G **E**
Verse 2	Now, look here Sal, I know you,
	A7
	Run down stocking and a wore out shoe.
	D **G**
	Honey, let me be your salty dog.
Chorus 2	*Repeat Chorus 1*
	G **E**
Verse 3	I was down in the wildwood sittin' on a log,
	A7
	Finger on the trigger and eye on a hog.
	D **G**
	Honey, let me be your salty dog.
Chorus 3	*Repeat Chorus 1*
	G **E**
Verse 4	I pulled the trigger and the gun set go,
	A7
	Shot fell over in Mexico.
	D **G**
	Honey, let me be your salty dog.
Chorus 4	*Repeat Chorus 1*

Shady Grove

Appalachian Folk Song

Cof - fee grows _ on the white oak trees, _

Verse 1

   C
Coffee grows on the white oak trees,

The river flows with brandy,

The rocks on the hill all covered with gold
   G   **C**
And the girls all sweeter than candy.

Chorus 1

   C
Shady grove, my little miss,

Shady grove my darlin',

Shady grove, my little miss,
G   **C**
Goin' back to Harlan.

Verse 2	C Well, I guess you think, my pretty little miss,
	I can't live without you.
	I'll let you know before I go G C I care a little a - bout you.
Chorus 2	*Repeat Chorus 1*
Verse 3	C Ev'ry time I go that road,
	It's always dark and cloudy.
	Ev'ry time I see that gal, G C I always tell her howdy.
Chorus 3	*Repeat Chorus 1*

Sitting on Top of the World

Words and Music by
Walter Jacobs and Lonnie Carter

Was in the spring, _____

(Capo 4th fret)

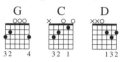

Verse 1

                 G
Was in the spring, ____ one sunny day,

        C   **G**
My good gal left me, she went away.

Chorus 1

        G
Now she's gone, and I don't worry.

              D   **G**
Lord, I'm sittin' on top of the world.

Verse 2

              G
She called me up ____ from down in El Paso.

           C   **G**
Said, "Come home daddy, I need you so."

Chorus 2

Repeat Chorus 1

Verse 3

        G
Ashes to ashes and dust to dust

        C   **G**
Show me a woman a man can trust.

Chorus 3	*Repeat Chorus 1*
Verse 4	G Mississippi River runs deep and wide. C G The gal I'm loving is on the other side.
Chorus 4	*Repeat Chorus 1*
Verse 5	G If you don't like my peaches don't you shake my tree. C G Stay out of my orchard and let the peaches be.
Chorus 5	*Repeat Chorus 1*
Verse 6	G Don't come to me holding out your hand. C G I'll get me a woman just like you got your man.
Chorus 6	*Repeat Chorus 1*

Sophronie

Words and Music by
Alton Delmore and D.C. Mullins

(Capo 4th fret)

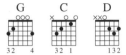

Chorus 1

    G
Love 'em and leave 'em,

    C
Kiss 'em and grieve 'em,

    D   **G**
That used to be my motto so high.

            C
'Till my Sophronie left me so lonely

      D   **G**
And now there's a teardrop in my eye.

Verse 1

         G   **C**
My Soph - ronie from Kentucky, she's found another man,

    D   **G**
I can't even kiss her, can't even hold her hand.

            C
The moon we used to love beneath is still up in the sky,

    D   **G**
So now I'm just a hotshot with a teardrop in my eye.

Chorus 2   *Repeat Chorus 1*

Verse 2

       G   C
'Till Gabriel blows his bugle, I'll be lovin' that sweet girl.

       D   G
She means more to me than the whole wide world.

                         C
I used to be a killer with the women, me oh my,

       D   G
But now I'm just a hotshot with a teardrop in my eye.

Chorus 3   *Repeat Chorus 1*

Verse 3

       G   C
I used to slay the pretty girls from Maine to Alabam',

       D   G
Love them very much at first, then I let them down.

                         C
I've seen so many pretty eyes been filled with bitter tears,

       D   G
Find them and forget them, but now I have my fears.

Chorus 4   *Repeat Chorus 1*

Turn Your Radio On

Words and Music by
Albert E. Brumley

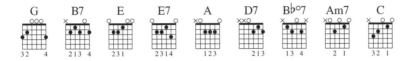

Melody:

Well, come and lis - ten in

G	B7	E	E7	A	D7	Bb°7	Am7	C
32 4	213 4	231	2314	123	213	13 4	2 1	32 1

Intro |G B7 E E7 |A D7 |G   Bb°7 Am7 |

Verse 1
      G N.C.   G
      Well, come and listen in to a radio station
                    C   G
      Where the mighty hosts of heaven sing.
                                  D7
      Turn your radio on, turn your radio on.
                    G
      If you want to feel those good vibrations
                    C   G
      Coming from the joy that His love can bring,
                           D7 G C
      Turn your radio on, turn your radio on.

	G C
Chorus 1	Turn your radio on and listen to the music in the air.

G   D7
Turn your radio on, heaven's glory share.

                     G   C
Turn your lights down low and listen to the Master's radio.

G   D7   G C G N.C.
Get in touch with God, turn your radio on.

Interlude   *Repeat Intro*

G N.C.   G
Verse 2   Don't you know that ev'ry - body has a radio receiver;

                     C   G
All you got to do is listen for the call.

                                    D7
Turn your radio on, turn your radio on.

                     G
If you listen in, you will be a believer

                     C   G
Leaning on the truths that were never false.

                                D7   G   C
Get in touch with God; turn your radio on.

Chorus 2   *Repeat Chorus 1*

Outro |G   B7   E   E7 |A   D7 |G   B♭°7 Am7 |G   ‖

Wabash Cannonball

Words and Music by
A.P. Carter

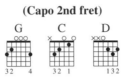

(Capo 2nd fret)

G C D

Verse 1

      G   C
From the great Atlantic Ocean to the wide Pacific shore

      D   G
From the queen of flowing mountains to the south bells by the shore.

                     C
She's mighty tall and handsome and known quite well by all.

D   G
She's the combination on the Wabash Cannon - ball.

Chorus 1

      G   C
Oh, listen to the jingle, the rumble and the roar,

       D   G
As she glides along the woodlands to the hills and by the shore.

                     C
Hear the mighty rush of the engine, hear the lonesome hobo's call.

      D   G
You're traveling through the jungle on the Wabash Cannon - ball.

Verse 2

           G   C

The Eastern states are dandy, so all the people say,

    D   G

From New York to St. Louis and Chicago by the way.

                                            C

From the hills of Minnesota, where the rippling waters fall,

    D   G

No chances can be taken on the Wabash Cannon - ball.

Chorus 2   *Repeat Chorus 1*

Verse 3

    G   C

She came down from Birmingham one cold December day.

       D   G

As she rolled into the station, you could hear all the people say

                                 C

There's gal from Tennessee, she's long and she's tall.

    D   G

She came down from Birmingham on the Wabash Cannon - ball.

Chorus 3   *Repeat Chorus 1*

Verse 4

    G   C

Here's to Daddy Claxton, may his name forever stand

       D   G

And always be remembered 'round the courts of Ala - bam'.

                                 C

His earthly race is over and the curtains 'round him fall.

    D   G

We'll carry him home to victory on the Wabash Cannon - ball.

Chorus 4   *Repeat Chorus 1*

What Would You Give in Exchange for Your Soul

Words and Music by
J.H. Carr and J.J. Berry

Verse 1

        F
Brother a - far from the Saviour today,

                    C
Risking your soul for the things that de - cay.

    F
Oh, if to - day God should call you away,

         C   **F**
What would you give in exchange for your soul?

Chorus 1

    F
What would you give, (In exchange) what would you give, (in exchange)

         C
What would you give in exchange for your soul?

    F
Oh, if to - day God should call you away,

         C   **F**
What would you give in exchange for your soul?

Verse 2	**F** Mercy is calling you,won't you give heed?

            F

Verse 2   Mercy is calling you,won't you give heed?

                 C

Must the dear Savior still tenderly plead?

          F

Risk not your soul, it is precious indeed.

        C   **F**

What would you give in exchange for your soul?

Chorus 2   *Repeat Chorus 1*

           F

Verse 3   More than the silver and gold of this earth,

           C

More than all jewels a spirit is worth.

       F

God the Cre - ator has given you birth.

        C   **F**

What would you give in exchange for your soul?

Chorus 3   *Repeat Chorus 1*

With Body and Soul

Words and Music by
Virginia Stauffer

Melody:

See that train come a - round

(Capo 2nd fret)

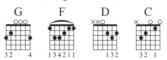

G   F   D   C

| | | | |
| Intro | N.C. |G | | | | | | | | | |

Intro N.C. |G | | | | | | | | |

Verse 1

     G   F   G
See that train come a - round the bend

                 F   D
Carrying the one ___ that I love.

     G   C   G
Her beautiful body is still here on earth,

                D   G
But her soul has been called above.

Chorus 1

     G   F   G   C
Body and soul, body and soul,

     G
That's how she loved me

         D   G
With body and soul.

Verse 2

G F   G
Her beautiful hair was the purest of gold,

      F   D
Her eyes were blue ___ as the sea,

  G   F G
Her lips were the col - or of summer's red rose,

       D   G
And she promised she would always love me.

Chorus 2   *Repeat Chorus 1*

Verse 3

G F G
To - morrow as the sun sinks low

      F   D
The shadows will cover her face.

  G   F   G
Her last sun goes down as she's laid beneath the ground

       D   G
And my teardrops are fallin' like rain.

Chorus 3

G F G   C
Body and soul, body and soul,

G
That's how she loved me

  D   G
With body and soul.

That's how she loved me

  D   G
With body and soul.

Working on a Building

Traditional

If I was a gam - bler,

(Capo 2nd fret)

Intro
| G | D | G | | |

Verse 1

G
If I was a gambler, I tell you what I would do,

                                D   **G**
I'd quit my gamblin' and I'd work on the building too.

Chorus 1

                    G
I'm working on a building, I'm working on a building.

                            D   **G**
I'm working on a building for my Lord, for my Lord.

It's a holy ghost building, it's a holy ghost building.

                            D   **G**
It's a holy ghost building, for my Lord, for my Lord.

Solo 1	|G	|	|	|	|
	|	|D	|G	|	|
	|	|	|	|	|
	|	|D	|G	|	|

Verse 2

    G
    If I was a drunkard, I tell you what I would do,

                        D   **G**
I'd quit my drinkin' and I'd work on the building too.

Chorus 2   *Repeat Chorus 1*

Solo 2   *Repeat Solo 1*

Verse 3

    G
    If I was a preacher, I tell you what I would do,

                        D   **G**
I'd keep on preachin' and I'd work on the building too.

Chorus 3   *Repeat Chorus 1*

The Wreck of the Old '97

Words and Music by Henry Whitter,
Charles Noell and Fred Lewey

Melody:

Well, they gave him his or - ders

(Capo 2nd fret)

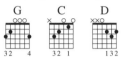

G   C   D

Verse 1

        G   **C**
Well, they gave him his orders in Monroe, Virginia

        G   **D**
Saying Steve, you're way behind time.

        G   **C**
This is not thirty-eight, but it's old ninety-seven,

        G   **D**   **G**
You must put her into Spencer on time.

Verse 2

        G   **C**
Well, he turned around, and said to his fireman,

    G   **D**
"Shovel in a little more coal.

     G   **C**
And when we cross this big wide mountain,

     G   **D**   **G**
We'll watch old ninty-seven roll."

Verse 3
```
       G                        C
It's a mighty rough road from Lynchburg to Danville,

       G                   D
And lined on a three-mile grade.

       G                   C
It's on that grade that he lost his air brakes,

       G       D       G
You see what a jump he made.
```

Verse 4
```
          G                              C
They were going down grade making ninety miles an hour

          G                 D
When his whistle broke into a scream.

       G                       C
He was found in a wreck with his hand on the throttle,

       G       D       G
Was scalded to death by the steam.
```

Verse 5
```
          G            C
Then a telegram came to Washington City,

       G       D
And this is how it read:

       G                  C
The brave engineer that run old ninety-seven

       G       D       G
Is lying in old Danville dead.
```

Verse 6
```
       G            C
Now all you ladies need take warning

       G              D
From the time now and learn,

       G                          C
Never speak harsh words to your true loving husband,

       G            D       G
He may leave you and never re - turn.
```

Once More

Words and Music by
Robert Owens

Once more, _____ to be _ with

D   G   C

Intro | D | | G | |

Chorus 1

           G
Once more, to be with you, dear,
               D
Just for to - night, to hold you tight.
          G   C
Once more, I'd give a for - tune,
              G   D   G
If I could see you   once more.

Verse

           G   C
For - get the past, this hurt can't last,
               G   D   G D
Oh, I don't want it to keep us a - part.
          G   D   G   C
Your love I'll crave, I'll be your slave
              G   D   G
If you'll just give me all of your heart.

Chorus 2

           G
Once more, to be with you, dear,
               D
Just for to - night, to hold you tight.
          G   C
Once more, I'd give a for - tune,
              G   D   G
If I could see you   once more.
N.C.   G
Once more.